Unstoppable

A Guide to Reclaiming Power and Creating Your Own Path

© 2025 Jill Miller & Janet "Toni" Federico

All rights reserved. No part of this publication may be reproduced or transmitted in any form or by any means, electronic or mechanical, including photocopying, recording, or any information storage or retrieval system, without prior permission in writing from the author and illustrator.

No responsibility for loss caused to any individual or organization acting on or refraining from action as a result of this publication is accepted by the author or the illustrator.

ISBN: 979-8-9866863-2-5 - Paperback
ISBN: 979-8-9866863-3-2 - Digital Online

Written by: Jill D. Miller
Designed and Typset by Toni Federico
Illustrated by Toni Federico

Dedication

This book is dedicated to:

Those who think you've lost something along the way, only to find out you really haven't.

Those who are learning to love themselves unconditionally.

Those who just need a reminder about what a badass you are.

Because you are UNSTOPPABLE. PERIOD.

Introduction

I'll give it to you straight: this book won't fix your life. No tidy formulas. No one-size-fits-all blueprint. No fairy godmother showing up to grant your three wishes. That's not how change works—and deep down, you already know it.

What this book offers: a crowbar.

Inside these pages are rebellious experiments, brutally honest prompts, and the occasional nudge (okay, shove) to help you pry loose the stories that keep you stuck. It's not about waiting to feel ready; it's about moving before you talk yourself out of it.

Waiting for the perfect time, the flawless plan, or for life to finally get easier is exhausting—and the moment never comes. The truth is, no one is coming to the rescue. Waiting is just another way of staying the same.

Consider this an invitation to treat this book like a workshop. Mark it up. Dog-ear the corners. Try the experiments, even the weird ones. Some will work; others won't. That's the point.

This workbook is divided into four parts:

→ **Action**: Challenge the status quo and spark the hard conversations.

→ **Connection**: Shift the way you engage with the world and make it a better place.

→ **Inspiration**: Jolt your perspective and see what's possible.

→ **Mindset**: Question your own thinking and expand your worldview.

There's no right way to move through it. Start at the beginning or skip around—you're in charge.

Some experiments are quick one-offs; others work best if you repeat them every day for a week. When the week's up, take a breath, look back, and jot down what happened. Which experiments sparked something in you? Those are the ones to keep—turn them into habits that keep the magic flowing.

And if it all feels overwhelming? Start with just one experiment a week. That's enough. You decide when to start, when to stop, and when to move on.

The hardest part isn't motivation—it's follow-through. This book can't do the work for you, but it will give you the tools, the questions, and the occasional push to make things happen.

Because once you stop waiting and start moving?

You are pure, glorious chaos—and the world better watch out.

Let's begin.

Action

Embrace your unstoppable self by challenging the status quo, adding a touch of spice to your life, celebrating what makes you you, and sparking the conversations that matter.

Take Action
Pick an adventurous Action Challenge and take on at least one activity on the list right away. If you're feeling bold, why not tackle all three? Get ready to step out of your comfort zone—soak up fresh knowledge, conquer tricky scenarios, and level up your skill set!

ACTION

Smash The Patriarchy

Question and transform systems that prioritize masculinity over femininity, championing women's equal status in society.

Take Action...

- Splurge at a local, woman-owned business.
- Don't fake orgasms.
- Jot down where you've let inequality sneak in and called it "normal."

Your Thoughts

ACTION

Speak With Power

If your voice had no power, no one would try to silence you. Don't undermine your credibility and hand over your power in an effort to be seen as a "nice girl."

Take Action...

- Stop apologizing and save the "sorry" for real boo-boos.
- Communicate with confidence by taking minimizing words like "sort of," "maybe," and "just" out of your conversations.
- Spread compliments and congratulations whenever you can.

Your Thoughts

ACTION

Celebrate Your Wins!

Noticing even the little victories uplifts your spirits and helps you pause to truly appreciate how far you've come.

Take Action...

- Treat yourself to some blooms.
- Bust out a victory dance.
- Create a sticker chart to mark milestones and treat yourself to a prize once it's filled.

Your Thoughts

ACTION

Be A Day Maker

Change the world simply by making someone's day. It doesn't need to be a stranger. People we know need help, too. Rather than random acts of kindness, plan intentional acts of goodwill.

Take Action...

- Shower deserving folks with a compliment that'll make their day.
- Serve up a warm meal or refreshing water for someone in need.
- Surprise someone you know by unexpectedly showing them kindness.

Your Thoughts

ACTION

Unleash Your Inner Superhero!

You are more powerful than you realize. Unleash the unique strengths and qualities that define you and take small steps to create a limitless life.

Take Action...

- Make a list of your super skills and passions.
- Bring out your brilliance by making time each day to use your talents.
- Pick one of your super skills and find a bold new way to use it.

Your Thoughts

ACTION

Savor The Moment

Find joy in the little things! Gain a deeper appreciation for life's simple pleasures by living in the moment and truly enjoying what's happening around you.

Take Action...

- Practice the fine dining art of savoring every tasty morsel.
- Embark on a vibrant color walk, letting your chosen hue lead the way.
- Give your eyes a break from all those pixels with a screen vacation.

Your Thoughts

ACTION

Sprinkle Kindness Like Confetti!

Create a ripple effect and make the world a better place by actively choosing to be kind and compassionate toward others in your words and deeds.

Take Action...

- Surprise someone with a secret good deed and tell no one.
- Clean up your neighborhood as you stroll.
- Roll up your sleeves and volunteer in your community.

Your Thoughts

ACTION

Take a Bold Leap Beyond Your Cozy Comfort Zone

Get intentional about challenging yourself beyond what feels safe and familiar. This is where magical growth happens, building confidence and broadening horizons.

Take Action...

- Confront a fear head-on.
- Master a fresh skill.
- Introduce yourself to someone you don't know.

Your Thoughts

ACTION

Embark on an Adventure!

Break free from the stupor of the status quo and wake up to unlimited possibilities by exploring a new way.

Take Action...

- Dive into a book, podcast, or show from a world you've never explored before.
- Say yes to the scenic route and take the long way on purpose.
- Shake things up and strut your stuff in a whole new style.

Your Thoughts

ACTION

Let Your Imagination Run Wild

Celebrate the joys of life and reclaim childish wonder through creation and play.

Take Action...

- Let your pen dance in a doodle drawing session.
- Try out being someone else by slipping into a whole new persona for a day.
- Embrace your inner fashionista with a dress-up extravaganza.

Your Thoughts

ACTION

Treat Yourself to a Solo Date Night

Manifest more self-love by spending some cherished moments by yourself, no matter what your relationship status.

Take Action...

- Belt out a love ballad to your reflection in the mirror.
- Catch a flick or enjoy a play-solo.
- Treat yourself to some fresh batteries or a snazzy personal massager.

Your Thoughts

ACTION

Amp Up That Mood

Try on some simple approaches to lift your spirits and change how you feel about life.

Take Action...

- Soak in some sunshine, and don't forget sunblock!
- Wiggle those toes in the grass.
- Practice the art of resting happy face.

Your Thoughts

ACTION

Refuse to Be Invisible

Sparkle like the brilliant gem you were destined to be, and no one will be able to overlook your shine.

Take Action...

- Go somewhere you feel out of place.
- Be bold by voicing your thoughts and throwing questions out there.
- Strut your stuff like you own the runway.

Your Thoughts

Play devil's advocate ...

Embracing perseverance usually means daring to take risks that nudge us beyond our comfort zones. By training our brains to feel at ease with discomfort, we're making incredible strides toward becoming truly unstoppable.

Your Thoughts

- Which of the actions you completed made you feel most uncomfortable?
- Which action was too uncomfortable to try?
- What do you think this discomfort is telling you?
- Is there another way to complete the action that works better for you?

_____
_____
_____
_____
_____
_____
_____
_____
_____
_____
_____
_____
_____
_____
_____
_____

Connection

Broaden your perspective, strengthen your relationships, and create a positive impact to make your life and the world around you richer, kinder, and more connected.

Get Connected

Explore a Connection Challenge to engage with the people around you—your community, your loved ones, your inner child, the natural world, or even a budding new passion. Strengthening these ties builds a sense of belonging that grounds you through life's highs and lows—and adds more joy to life.

CONNECTION

Forge a Bond With Another Generation

It's all too common to drift apart from those we are connected to, whether by blood or choice. Don't wait for the next celebration or crisis to be reunited. Instead, reach out to someone from a different generation to gain a fresh perspective.

Take Action...

Choose a loved one from another age group and connect with them through a visit, phone call, text, or letter to catch up and strengthen your bond.

Your Thoughts

CONNECTION

Patch Up a Relationship

Everybody makes mistakes now and then. Sometimes, the golden ticket to moving ahead is to own up to our blunders and roll up our sleeves to fix the mess. Rebuilding trust and patching up relationships takes a bit more than just a simple apology.

Take Action...

Write a heartfelt letter to someone you'd love to reconnect with or smooth over past disagreements. Come clean about what happened and lay out your game plan for a fresh start. It's up to you whether you choose to read it to them, hit send, or even toss it into the flames.

Your Thoughts

CONNECTION

Spark Change In Your Community

Local government meetings play a major role in shaping public policy by allowing civil servants to hear what matters most to the community. By showing up and sharing your thoughts, you can be the spark that ignites change and steer society in a new direction, just by being there. Your voice matters, so grab that mic and get involved!

Take Action...

Attend online or in-person local government meetings, such as those held by the school board, city council, district advisory boards, county council, or statehouse. Consider how you can make your voice heard.

CONNECTION

Be a Friendly Face

Being friendly with our neighbors champions a robust sense of community, boosts personal safety, gives us a shoulder to lean on when times get tough, and helps us form lasting friendships. You don't need a superhero cape to be a great neighbor. A simple "hello" and a friendly check-in can work wonders in creating kindhearted connections.

Take Action...

There are so many ways to help our neighbors. Whether it's cleaning up after a storm or keeping an eye on their place while they're off on adventures, there's no shortage of good deeds. So, roll up your sleeves and lend a hand or do something kind just for the fun of it.

Your Thoughts

CONNECTION

Discover Fresh Horizons

Connecting with locals and fellow wanderers to soak up their unique vibes is the ultimate treasure of any adventure. You don't need to hop on a plane to make a friend from far-off lands. Dive into the digital world of pen-pal platforms where you can match with folks who share your passions and preferred chat styles. Adventure awaits in your inbox!

Take Action...

Make a new bestie across the miles and become a pen pal with someone from another state or even a whole different country!

Your Thoughts

CONNECTION

Be Generous with Praise

Give a stranger a genuine, heartfelt compliment, and notice how it makes both of you feel. Spread positivity by speaking up about what you love in others' fabulous choices. The lovely feelings you create by lifting someone up will bounce right back to you like a boomerang of happiness.

Take Action...

Drop a genuine, heartfelt compliment on a stranger and notice the magic unfold for both of you.

Your Thoughts

CONNECTION

Uncover Mother Nature's Treasures

Breathe in that sweet, sweet, fresh air and get moving. Feeling that warm, fuzzy connection with Mother Nature is like a big hug for our souls, boosting our happiness and well-being!

Take Action...

Lace up those walking shoes and hit the great outdoors. Discover little treasures that scream "YOU!" Then, spin a story about your find through pictures, words, or video magic. Dive into the whys and whatnots of your choice and what it means to you.

Your Thoughts

CONNECTION

Dust Off A Forgotten Talent

Sometimes, we drift away from the skills we once loved to practice. Perhaps our passions led us on unexpected detours, or work and stress overshadowed our hobbies. But you can always rediscover those forgotten talents and jump back in whenever inspiration strikes you again.

Take Action...

Try on an old skill you once delighted in and see if it still puts a wiggle in your waggle. Does it still spark joy or just leave you feeling uninspired?

Your Thoughts

CONNECTION

Polish Your Battle Armor

Even the wildest roller coasters of life, with their loops of trauma and bumps of challenge, can launch us into amazing transformations. Those unexpected skills we've been secretly honing—like becoming boundary-setting ninjas or self-protection wizards—are superpowers we should totally celebrate, not overlook!

Take Action...

Craft a list of the super skills you've snagged while battling through tough times in your history.

Your Thoughts

CONNECTION

Rewind a Blissful Finale

Sometimes, the changes we dread the most turn out to be the best plot twists in our life's story. We get so caught up in dodging the discomfort that we forget to peek at the treasure chest of gains waiting on the other side.

Take Action...

Write up a list of those nerve-wracking changes that had you sweating bullets at first but, in the end, turned out to be your ticket to happiness.

Your Thoughts

CONNECTION

Nurture Your Younger You

Our inner child is like a mischievous sprite running wild inside us, pulling at our emotions and throwing tantrums, whether we realize it or not. Tapping into that youthful spirit is a magical remedy, no matter how many candles are on your birthday cake.

Take Action...

Compose a sweet, heartwarming pep talk you wish someone had whispered in your ear back in the day. Then read them like a heartfelt serenade to your younger self or even a cute photo of you from that time. Give that little version of you all the unconditional love they crave.

Your Thoughts

CONNECTION

Pause For a Mindful Moment

Soak in some nature vibes and reconnect with your inner self while enjoying the great outdoors. Engage your senses and dive into the moment to embrace the enchantment. Nature's a buffet for your senses—dig in!

Take Action...

Play a little game with your senses: spot five things that catch your eye, explore four textures that intrigue your fingers, listen for three sounds serenading your ears, sniff out two delightful scents, and savor one delicious taste. Take a moment to reflect on your feelings before and after, and notice the changes.

Your Thoughts

CONNECTION

Cuddle Up With a Cozy Companion

Being in the furry (or scaly) presence of animals lifts our spirits, deepens compassion, strengthens social bonds, and sparks a flood of love. Whether you're snuggling with your own pets, volunteering at a shelter, rescuing critters, loving on a friend's pet, or browsing famous animals online, the connections you form are simply pawesome.

Take Action...

Snuggle up with your furry friend for some top-notch cuddle sessions, or roll up your sleeves and lend a paw at a local animal rescue.

Your Thoughts

Play devil's advocate ...

Not everyone feels comfortable making connections and meeting strangers out in the wild. Some of us would rather wrestle a raccoon than attend a networking event. But connection doesn't always require a crowd—just curiosity and a little courage.

Your Thoughts

- When do you feel most safe and yourself around others?
- What kinds of interactions leave you feeling energized instead of drained?
- What stops you from reaching out—even when part of you wants to?
- What are some ways you can make social connections without it feeling risky?

Inspiration

Sometimes the best inspiration comes in a single sentence. One powerful quote can shift your mindset, spark a fresh idea, or simply remind you you're not alone.

Get Inspired
Activate a new way of seeing with an *Inspiration Challenge*: pick a quote and let the accompanying question guide you to tell a story, through images or words. Sometimes, all it takes is one new lens to change your whole perspective.

"A woman is like a tea bag - you never know how strong she is until she gets in hot water."

— Eleanor R.

TRY ME

Q. When have you been in hot water, and what did you learn?

Q: Where can you venture into new settings that weren't built for you?

Q: What are you doing to hold up your sisters?

Q: What have you achieved that wasn't supported?

Q: What is your superpower?

"Empty your cup, so that it may be filled" - Bruce Lee

Q: What are you holding onto that you need to let go of?

Q: What internal or external scar are you most proud of?

"Live by the joy suck rule. If something is sucking the joy out of your life, it has to go."

– Headmistress Jill Miller

Q: What is sucking the joy out of your life right now?

Q: Who is in your life that you don't feel safe sharing your vulnerabilities with?

Q: How or where do you question your power?

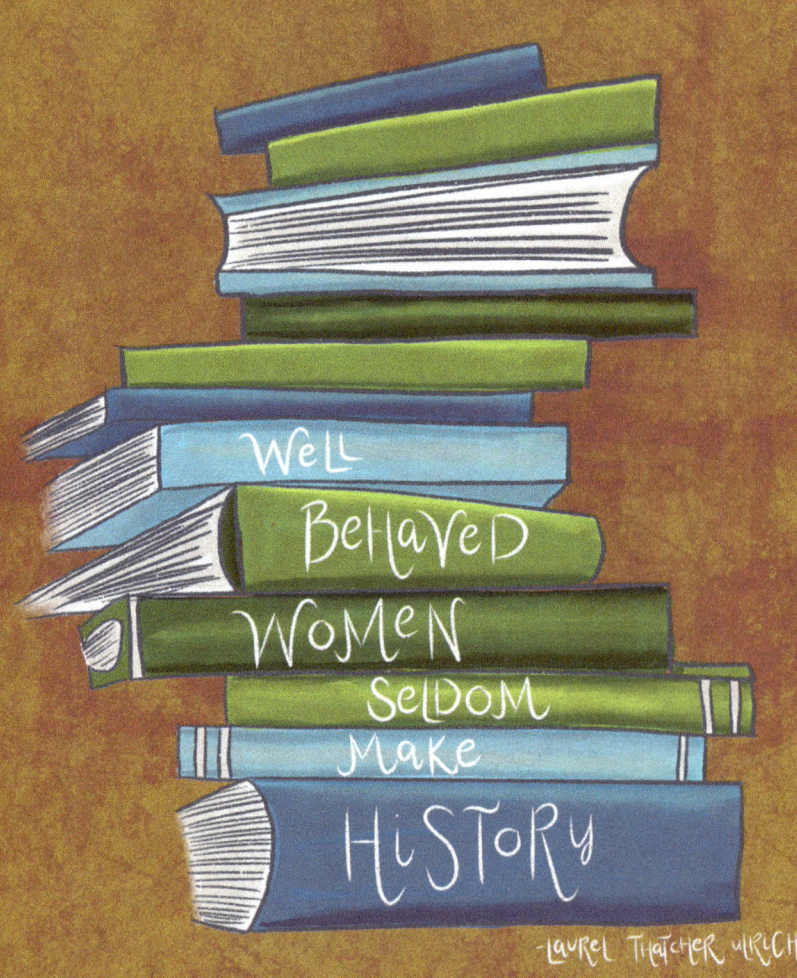

Q: Where are you holding yourself back out of fear of offending someone?

Q: What have you gained from the tough times you've experienced?

Play devil's advocate …

Real change usually takes more than a clever line—it takes context, action, and lived experience. Not every quote will crack open your worldview or light your creative fire—and that's okay. But when the right words hit at the right time? That's when the magic happens. So, maybe it's not about finding just the quote, but being open enough to let it move you when it does.

Your Thoughts

- Where do you find inspiration?
- If someone were to quote you, what would you want it to say?
- What's a quote that's stuck with you, and what does it mean to you?
- What words do you live by—and how do they shape your story?

Mindset

Test your way of thinking and explore how you see yourself and the world around you to unlock fresh perspectives, break free from old patterns, and create the life you truly want.

Challenge Yourself
Answer a call to adventure with a Mindset Challenge and let go of the dead weight, spark wild ideas about what's next, or simply remember how to play. These experiments invite you to pause, awaken old dreams, and reclaim your inner power to see what's possible and take meaningful steps toward the life you want.

MINDSET

Write a Review

Remember those book reports from your school days? Whether you were a fan or not, what you gained from writing the report will stick with you for a long time. Putting your thoughts on paper helps you untangle ideas and dive deeper into understanding.

Take Action...

Grab an article or a book on a subject that intrigues you and create a captivating review highlighting your discoveries. Bonus points if you share how you plan to incorporate that newfound knowledge into your life.

Your Thoughts

MINDSET

Create a Joy List

Happiness can be hard to pin down, so rather than chasing it, try focusing on joy. Joy lives in the moment and is easier to find than happiness. Even during tough times, connecting with feelings of joy has a ripple effect that reaches beyond the moment to broaden the mind and heal body and soul. Besides, one joyful moment invites another.

Take Action...

Grab your sparkliest notebook, colorful markers, and collection of stickers, and create a list of joyful moments from your past and all the fabulous things you're excited about in the future. Review the list often, repeat what makes you joyful, and keep adding more ideas.

Your Thoughts

MINDSET

Take Time to Reflect

Life is too short to keep making the same mistakes. One way to avoid these pesky pitfalls is through retrospection. By thinking about what we've learned, we can consider which of these lessons we want to keep and toss what we no longer need as we strut confidently into our fabulous futures.

Take Action...

Do a quick self-check anytime by jotting down your thoughts on these questions:

- What were the excellent highlights and the not-so-great lows?
- What lessons did I learn?
- Which lessons are coming along for the ride, and which ones can stay behind?
- What were my epic wins, and how will I celebrate them?

Your Thoughts

MINDSET

Create SMART Goals

When you have your eye on the prize, it's like wearing blinders to all the distractions, giving you a clear path and a forward focus. So, let's get SMART about it: plot out your plan with goals that are Specific, Measurable, Attainable (with a dash of challenge), Relevant, and Time-bound.

Take Action...

Choose a project that lights you up, then set a few short-term goals and one bold, long-term vision. Track your progress and check in with your plan regularly.

Your Thoughts

MINDSET

Let Go of a Grudge

Holding onto grudges and owed apologies keeps you anchored in the past. Don't be a Bitter Betty—release that baggage! Even if others stay stuck, you have the power to free yourself. Letting go, finding peace, and forgiving are gifts you give yourself as well as others. While acceptance and forgiveness don't always lead to reunion, they can offer a sense of release. And sometimes, that's the first step toward healing your own heart.

Take Action...

Which of your relationships are weighed down by hurt or resentment? Take some time to reflect on what happened, what was said, what wasn't, and how it left its mark. Write it out, not to relive the pain, but to understand it.

Your Thoughts

MINDSET

Plan a Trip

Just thinking about a new adventure can spark a burst of child-like excitement, even if you never step foot outside your door. The sweet anticipation from planning a trip gives a mood boost that outlasts the journey itself. Whether your getaway is a whirlwind two-day jaunt or a dreamy two-month escapade, mapping out your dream vacation will bring you one step closer to your happy place.

Take Action...

Ignite your wild imagination and embark on a thrilling quest to create the adventure of your dreams. Dive into a sea of endless possibilities and sketch out your plans with words, pictures, or collages as vibrant and detailed as you can dream. Add a dash of reality by estimating what it'll cost to turn that dream into a reality.

Your Thoughts

MINDSET

Plan a Trip

Just thinking about a new adventure can spark a burst of child-like excitement, even if you never step foot outside your door. The sweet anticipation from planning a trip gives a mood boost that outlasts the journey itself. Whether your getaway is a whirlwind two-day jaunt or a dreamy two-month escapade, mapping out your dream vacation will bring you one step closer to your happy place.

Take Action...

Ignite your wild imagination and embark on a thrilling quest to create the adventure of your dreams. Dive into a sea of endless possibilities and sketch out your plans with words, pictures, or collages as vibrant and detailed as you can dream. Add a dash of reality by estimating what it'll cost to turn that dream into a reality.

Your Thoughts

MINDSET

Change Something

Ever feel like you're spinning on a never-ending hamster wheel, stuck in the daily grind? Instead of just grinning and bearing it, maybe it's time to shake up your snow globe. When you finally pause and spot the joy suckers, you can flex those mental muscles and make small shifts that lead to big, meaningful change.

Take Action...

Grab a moment to zero in on a joy-draining culprit and start plotting your escape. Write down or doodle what you'll ditch and what you'll gain by switching things up or staying put —both the good and the not-so-good. Then, picture your future self, living the dream, and outline the tiny steps to get there. Make it a plan to take a little action every day, and soon, you'll be strutting toward your fabulous new life.

Your Thoughts

MINDSET

Assess Your Values

The principles and values we hold dear are like our personal GPS, steering us through life's wild ride. When you nail down your ideals, you can dodge bad choices and regrets like a pro, making decisions that fit you like a glove. Diving into the values you admire in others will help you discover the hidden gems within yourself.

Take Action...

Grab some paper and colorful markers and get ready for some soul-searching. Ask yourself:

- Who do I admire most, and why?
- Who are my heroes (from the past or present), and what makes them legendary in my eyes?
- What or who uplifts and inspires me?

Once you've connected with the traits you most admire, choose three or four to cherish and let them be your guiding stars on this cosmic journey of life.

Your Thoughts

MINDSET

Mental Inventorying

Most of the 50,000 thoughts we have each day are just busy bees buzzing around our to-do lists. But feeling busy doesn't always mean we're actually getting anything done. Every choice we make about how to spend our time is really a decision about how much of our most precious resource—our energy—we're giving away. The trouble is, we often pretend we have an endless supply and end up feeling like a drained battery.

Take Action...

Combat decision fatigue and clear some mental clutter by doing a mental inventory. Write down everything you're juggling, think you should be juggling, and secretly wish you were juggling. Then scan your list with curiosity—ask yourself why each item is getting your time and energy. Is it essential? Does it truly matter to you or someone you care about? If not, give yourself permission to cross that distraction off your list and let it go.

Your Thoughts

MINDSET

Think Like a Kid

One of the saddest parts of growing up is forgetting how to play. We believe seriousness equals success, treating mistakes as flaws instead of part of the process. Remembering to play reconnects us to the freedom, curiosity, and fun of our childhood. Play brings joy, sparks creativity, heals wounds, and reminds us that growth can be light, bold, and fun.

Take Action...

Remember what it was like to be young and explore the world with wonder. Write on strips of paper what you loved as a child—games, toys, activities, places—and put them in a jar. When you need a mood boost, draw a slip and celebrate that memory by doing, writing, creating, or planning to relive it.

Your Thoughts

MINDSET

Your "Someday" Wish

We all have an elusive "someday" wish—things we'll get to someday when the stars align and everything feels just right. We keep pushing our heart's desires aside, waiting for that perfect moment—if it ever arrives. Could it be a matter of timing, or is it just that scary monster lurking outside our comfort zone?

Take Action...

What "someday" wish has been stuck in your brain? Picture it as a fairy tale, where you're the princess on the brink of an epic escapade. What wild challenges lie ahead in your quest for glory? How will you slay those metaphorical monsters and land that happily ever after? Spin your yarn through words or doodles, then think about how to turn it into a "based on a true story" adventure!

Your Thoughts

MINDSET

Write Your Younger Self

Tucked away in the corners of our hearts is our inner child, just waiting to materialize when those stubborn, unhealed childhood memories come back to haunt us. To let go of the old reactions we learned as kids, we can reconnect with our inner child and shower ourselves with the love, compassion, and support we truly deserved back then.

Take Action...

Take a stroll down memory lane to that moment when life felt like a tough playground. With all your grown-up wisdom, picture that little one standing right before you. What would you say to her? Grab a pen, pour your heart out in a loving letter, sprinkle in some admiration, and let the love flow to dish out the kind advice you wish she had back in the day.

Your Thoughts

MINDSET

You're a Superhero

We think of superpowers as out-of-this-world abilities, by those either donning capes as superheroes or twirling mustaches as supervillains. But superpowers don't have to be all about capes and chaos. We all have our own slice of power pie that we can wield for good, not evil! By discovering our values, passions, talents, and strengths, we can transform those traits into our very own superpowers.

Take Action...

What are your superhero skills? Jot down your values, passions, talents, and strengths and line them up like a team of Avengers! Spot the patterns, find the overlaps, and connect the dots to unveil your epic superpower!

Your Thoughts

Play devil's advocate ...

Sometimes the biggest shift comes from slowing down. Growth isn't always about movement. It can look like stillness, reflection, or simply being present. Even the smallest mindset shift—a small spark of clarity or curiosity can gently steer your life in a new direction. You don't need a full reset. Just be open to the possibility that something new is waiting, and trust yourself enough to take one honest step toward it.

Your Thoughts

- What part of my past have I been trying to "let go of" that might actually hold wisdom I haven't fully acknowledged?
- Where am I feeling resistance to change, and what could that resistance be trying to teach me?
- What if nothing needed to be "fixed" about me right now? How would that shift the way I show up in my life?
- What small, compassionate shift in thinking could help me feel more at peace right now?

About Us

Jill D. Miller is dedicated to helping people grow—boldly, authentically, and on their own terms. Through her consulting company, Creative Solutions, she's guided entrepreneurs since 1998, launching businesses that are as original and spirited as their founders.

A natural teacher, Jill discovered her love for sparking transformation as a corporate trainer and now channels it as an adjunct professor at Wichita State University. As Headmistress of the Finishing School for Modern Women, she's worked with thousands of women since 2015, challenging them to smash limitations, embrace their power, and keep moving forward.

She's also the founder of the Badass Women of Wichita Alliance, a vibrant community that gathers regularly to connect, uplift local nonprofits, and grow a little more "badass" every day. Her debut book, Never Finished: Practical Advice for Modern Women to Inspire Your Fierce, Authentic Self (2022), sprang from years of writing a blog that encouraged readers to question the rules and write their own and is now available as an audiobook through Patreon.

Deeply rooted in her Wichita community, Jill leads cultural and women's organizations, volunteers with unflagging enthusiasm, and is a fixture at local arts and cultural events. When she's not teaching, organizing, or stirring up new ideas, she loves unwinding at home with her miniature rescue poodle, Jack.

Learn more at finishingschoolformodernwomen.com

Toni Federico, MBA, PMP, MFA is a freelance illustrator, designer, podcaster, and creative coach. Working digitally in Procreate, Illustrator, and Photoshop, Toni creates bold, whimsical, and sophisticated designs that reimagine the familiar in unexpected ways. From playful surface patterns to evocative illustrations, her work blends emotional storytelling with a distinctive, design-forward aesthetic.

A certified Project Management Professional (PMP) with three decades of experience, Toni helps artists and creative entrepreneurs bring structure to their chaos through project management and course design coaching. She teaches artists how to make art, meet deadlines, and stay sane—because creativity thrives best when it's got a plan.

Toni is also the co-host of Two Cranky Creatives, a no-BS podcast for working artists who crave real talk about creative careers, and co-leads Graphics Gang, her Patreon community where she shares feedback, creative challenges, and behind-the-scenes peeks into her art practice.

Whether she's designing for clients, mentoring creatives, or developing a new class, Toni's mission is the same: to make art that feels alive—art that's joyful, thoughtful, and just a little rebellious. Her work invites you to slow down, find your spark, and maybe laugh at the beautiful mess of being creative.

Find Toni at owlmedicinedesigns.com or on the socials @owlmedicinedesign

www.ingramcontent.com/pod-product-compliance
Lightning Source LLC
Chambersburg PA
CBHW052130030426
42337CB00028B/5094